The Deep End: Animal Life Underwater

I0793870

Great White Shark

by Jen Green

Consultants:

John E. McCosker, PhD
Chair of Aquatic Biology, California Academy of Sciences

Maureen Flannery, MS
Ornithology and Mammalogy Collection Manager, California Academy of Sciences

Wallace J. Nichols, PhD
Research Associate, California Academy of Sciences

BEARPORT PUBLISHING

New York, New York

Credits

Cover, © David Fleetham/Visuals Unlimited/Corbis; 3, © Norbert Probst/FLPA; 4–5, © Barcroft Media; 6, © Ingo Arndt/Minden Pictures/FLPA; 7, © Image Source/Corbis; 8–9, © Norbert Probst/FLPA; 10, © Joshua Haviv/Shutterstock; 11, © Mike Parry/Minden Pictures/FLPA; 12, © Mike Parry/Minden Pictures/Getty Images; 13, © iStockphoto/Thinkstock; 13TL, © David Wrobel/Visuals Unlimited/Corbis; 13TR, © Stephan Kerkhofs/Shutterstock; 13C, © Cho Ye Wah/Shutterstock; 13BR, © Franz Lanting/Corbis; 13BL, © Malcolm Schuyl/FLPA; 14–15, © Visuals Unlimited/Corbis; 16, © Steve & Ann Toon/Robert Harding World Imagery/Corbis; 17, © Mike Parry/Minden Pictures/FLPA; 18, © Franz Lanting/Corbis; 19, © Andy Murch/Visuals Unlimited/Getty Images; 20, © Randy Wilder/Monterey Bay Aquarium; 21, © Toby Hunt/Shutterstock; 22, © Wayne Lynch/All Canada Photos/Getty Images; 23TL, © Ocean/Corbis; 23TR, © David Yarrow/Getty Images; 23BR, © Randy Wilder/Monterey Bay Aquarium; 23BL, © Stubblefield Photography/Shutterstock; 24, © Fuse/Thinkstock.

Publisher: Kenn Goin
Editorial Director: Adam Siegel
Creative Director: Spencer Brinker
Photo Researcher: Brown Bear Books Ltd

Library of Congress Cataloging-in-Publication Data

Green, Jen.
Great white shark / By Jen Green.
p. cm. — (The deep end: animal life underwater)
Includes bibliographical references and index.
ISBN 978-1-61772-918-8 (library binding) — ISBN 1-61772-918-3 (library binding)
ISBN: 978-1-64280-810-0 (pbk.)
1. White shark—Juvenile literature. I. Title.
QL638.95.L3G755 2014
597.3'3—dc23
2013010869

For more information, write to Bearport Publishing, 5357 Penn Avenue South, Minneapolis MN 55419. Printed in the United States of America.

Contents

A Sudden Danger

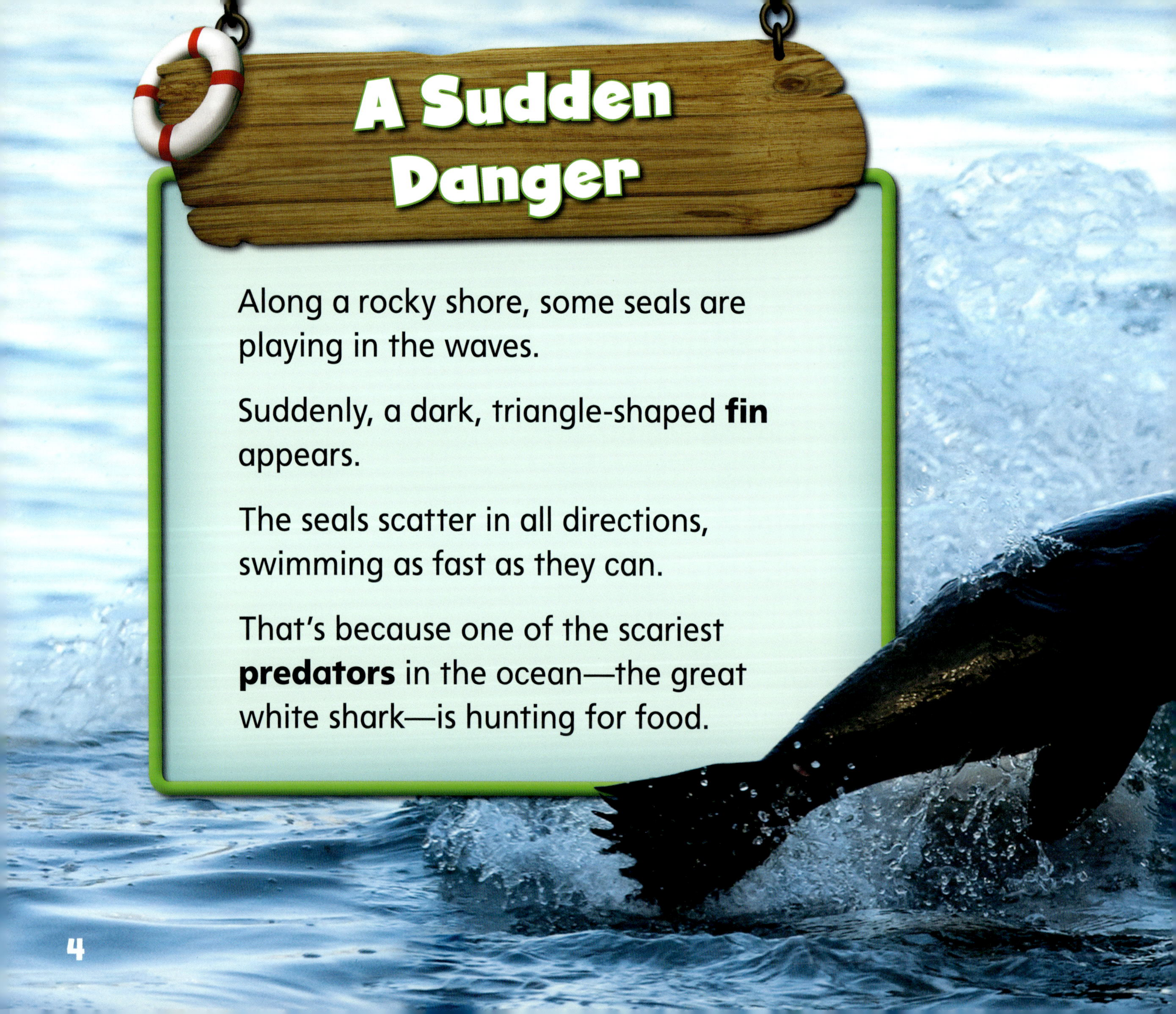

Along a rocky shore, some seals are playing in the waves.

Suddenly, a dark, triangle-shaped **fin** appears.

The seals scatter in all directions, swimming as fast as they can.

That's because one of the scariest **predators** in the ocean—the great white shark—is hunting for food.

Adult great white sharks can grow to 20 feet (6 m) in length—longer than three tall adult men lying head to toe. These sharks can weigh more than 2 tons (1.8 metric tons), or as much as an adult rhinoceros.

Meet the Great White Shark

About 370 different kinds of sharks live in the world's oceans.

All of these fish are meat-eaters.

Some sharks eat only tiny shrimp-like animals called krill.

The great white shark, however, is a fierce hunter of many sea creatures.

In fact, it's the largest predator among all the world's fish.

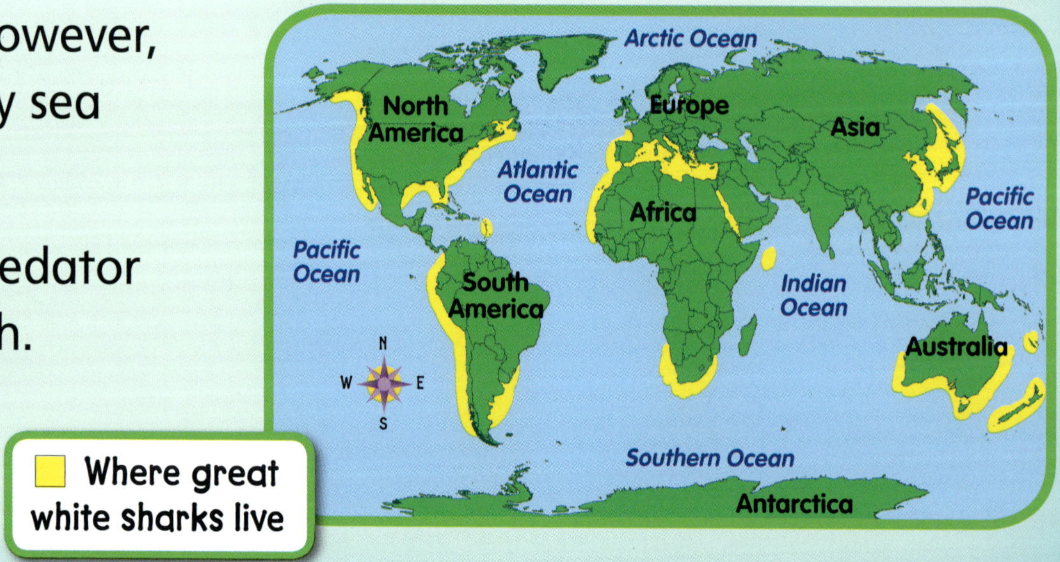

Great white sharks swim mainly in ocean waters that are close to land. However, some also swim long distances across the world's oceans.

Look at the shape of the shark's body. In what way might it help the shark be a good underwater hunter?

Champion Swimmers

The great white shark is one of the best swimmers in the sea.

With its long body and pointed nose, it slips smoothly through the water.

To swim forward, it moves its powerful tail from side to side.

To turn, it uses the large fins on its sides.

It also uses them to move up and down.

The fin on the shark's back keeps it from rolling over while it swims.

When they need to, great white sharks can swim more than 15 miles per hour (24 kph)—that's about three times faster than the fastest human swimmer.

Hiding in the Water

The great white shark has a dark back and a white belly.

Its coloring helps it hide as it hunts during the day.

Animals that swim above the shark can't see its dark back against the dark water below.

Animals that are below it can't see its white belly against the bright surface above.

As a result, the shark can swim right up to its **prey** without being seen.

The great white shark gets its name from its large size and the white coloring of its underside. It is often called "great white" for short.

What animals do you think a shark hunts and eats?

What's On the Menu?

Great whites swim around all day looking for food.

Seals are the favorite meal of adult sharks.

Young great whites will also eat crabs, fish, octopuses, squid, and penguins.

Sometimes sharks attack people, but these attacks are very rare. Some experts think that great whites go after humans because they mistake them for seals.

Shark Food

How do you think a shark finds its food?

Sharp Senses

Great whites have good eyesight.

Yet they also use other senses when they are hunting.

They have an excellent sense of smell.

This helps them find prey from a distance.

A shark's sense of touch helps it find food, too.

The shark can feel the ripples made by other swimming animals.

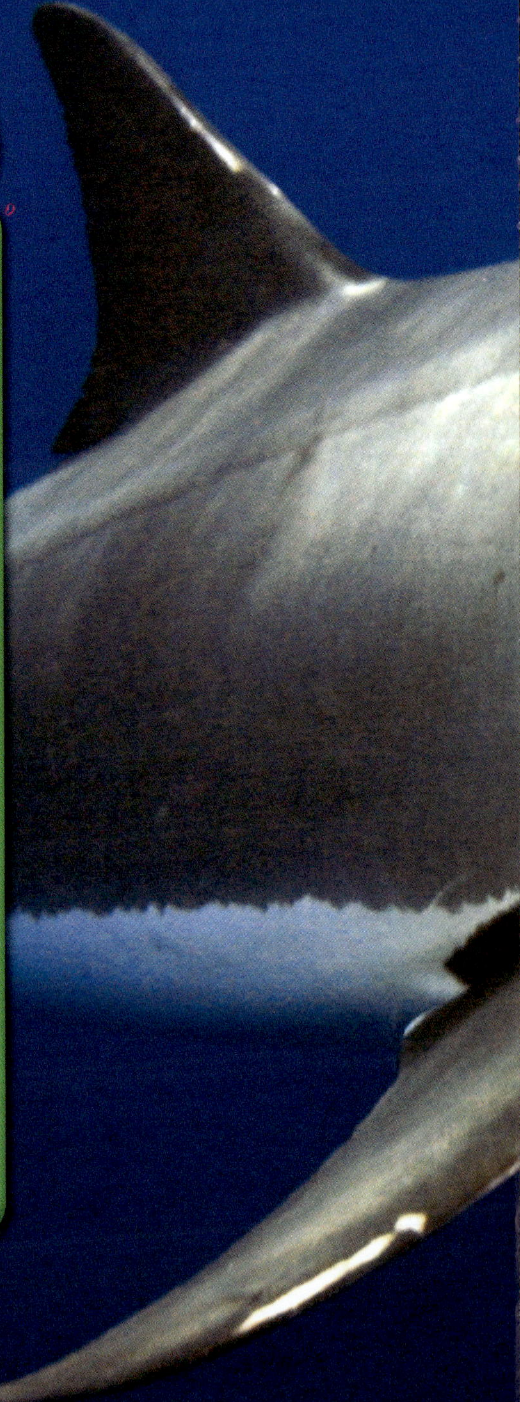

Great white sharks can smell the tiniest amounts of blood mixed in the water. The blood tells them if an injured animal is nearby.

Shark Attack!

A great white shark usually hunts just below the water's surface.

It quickly swims toward its prey.

Then the shark swims up from below to bite the sea creature.

If the prey is large, the shark tears off chunks of meat with its razor-sharp teeth.

If the prey is small, the shark swallows it whole.

A great white shark's teeth are very sharp. They can slice through skin, flesh, and even bone.

Shark Babies

Great whites are fish, but they don't start their lives the way most fish do.

Almost all kinds of fish hatch from eggs that their mothers lay in the water.

Great white sharks, however, hatch from eggs while they are still inside their mothers.

The babies grow and stay safe there.

Then, after about a year, the mothers give birth to tiny baby sharks.

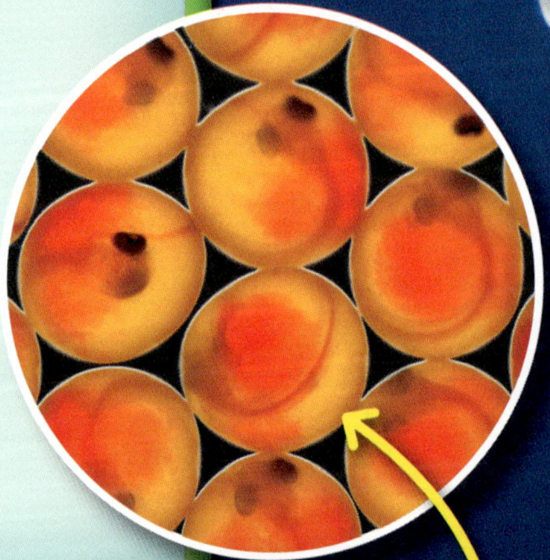

adult female great white shark

A female great white shark can give birth to up to 12 babies at one time.

What do you think a baby great white shark looks like?

Growing Up Underwater

Baby sharks are called **pups**.

They look a lot like adult sharks, but they are smaller.

As soon as pups are born, they are able to survive on their own.

The young sharks start out by hunting small fish and squid.

As they grow, they keep hunting almost anything they can grab with their sharp teeth.

Great white sharks are fully grown when they are around 15 years old. They can live for more than 30 years.

Science Lab

Be a Shark Scientist!

Imagine you are a scientist who studies great whites. Write a report to tell other people about them.

The information in this book will help you. Draw pictures to include in your report.

When you are finished, present your report to family and friends.

Use these words to write and talk about great white sharks:

smell eggs prey fish

hunting teeth hiding

Read the questions below and think about the answers.

You can include some of the information from your answers in your report.

- *What do great white sharks eat?*
- *How do they find their prey?*
- *How do great whites kill other animals?*
- *How do young sharks live?*

Science Words

fin (FIN) one of the pointed body parts that a shark uses to move or balance itself while swimming

predators (PRED-uh-turz) animals that hunt other animals for food

prey (PRAY) animals that are hunted and eaten by other animals

pups (PUPS) baby sharks

Index

Read More

Bodden, Valerie. *Sharks (Amazing Animals).* Mankato, MN: Creative Education (2010).

Cole, Joanna. *Hungry, Hungry Sharks.* New York: Random House (2009).

Pringle, Laurence. *Sharks! Strange and Wonderful.* Honesdale, PA: Boyds Mills Press (2008).

Learn More Online

To learn more about great white sharks, visit **www.bearportpublishing.com/TheDeepEnd**

About the Author

Jen Green has been interested in natural history since she was a child. She has written dozens of children's books on subjects as varied as raccoons, gophers, and termites. She loves walking in her native Sussex, England.